SEA LION

by CAROLINE ARNOLD
photographs by RICHARD HEWETT

MORROW JUNIOR BOOKS • *New York*

PHOTO CREDITS: Permission to use the following photographs is gratefully acknowledged: Arthur Arnold, pages 11 and 23.

The text type is 14-point Usherwood Medium.
1 2 3 4 5 6 7 8 9 10

Library of Congress Cataloging-in-Publication Data.   Arnold, Caroline.   Sea lion / Caroline Arnold; photographs by Richard Hewett.   p.   cm.   ISBN 0-688-12027-X (trade)—ISBN 0-688-12028-8 (library)   1. California sea lion—Juvenile literature. 2. Wildlife rescue—Juvenile literature. [1. California sea lion. 2. Sea lions. 3. Wildlife rescue.]   I. Hewett, Richard, ill.   II. Title.   QL737.P63A715   1994   599.74'6—dc20   93-27007   CIP   AC

.7975

Acknowledgments

We would like to express our appreciation to all of the people who helped us on this project. We especially thank Judi Jones, operations director, and the devoted volunteer staff at the Friends of the Sea Lion Marine Mammal Center in Laguna Beach, California (pictured above), for their assistance on this project. We also thank Don Zumwalt, director, and Pat Ryan, operations manager, at the Marine Mammal Care Center at Fort MacArthur in San Pedro, California, and the staff of Sea World California in San Diego for their help. Like other centers located elsewhere along the coasts of the United States, each of these facilities is devoted to rescuing and rehabilitating sick and injured sea animals. We would also like to thank Don Jim for his assistance and our editor, Andrea Curley, for her continued enthusiastic support.

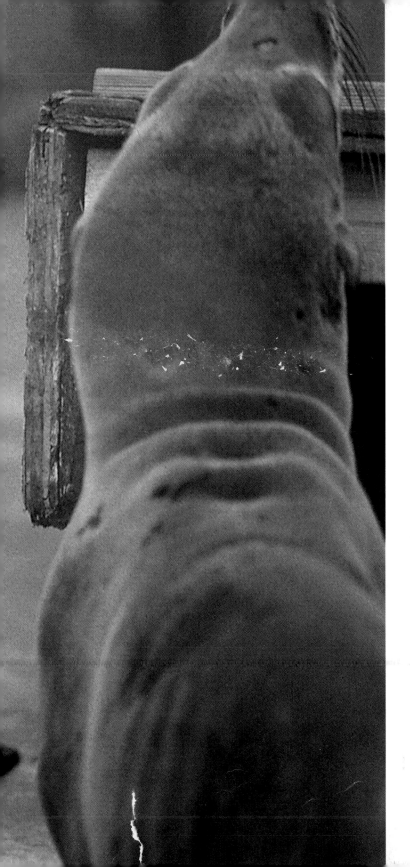

Moving forward on leathery flippers, Pumpkin and Piper peered through the fence of their enclosure. On the other side they could see two more young sea lions just like themselves. All around them, they could hear the noisy barking of other sea lions that lived at the Marine Mammal Center in southern California. Like Pumpkin and Piper, each of the animals had come to the center because it was sick or injured and needed help to survive.

Every year, hundreds of sea lions are found along the west coast of North America and are brought into shelters like the Marine Mammal Center. The staff members at each rescue center give them food, medical care, and a safe place to stay. The staff tries to bring the animals back to health as quickly as possible so that they can be returned to the wild to live on their own.

Recently, an increasing number of sea lions and other sea mammals have been brought to shelters. Changing weather conditions, pollution, over-fishing, and a growth in the sea lion population all have contributed to a reduction in the supply of fish and other foods that sea lions eat. When animals do not get enough to eat, they find it harder to fend for themselves and often become weak or sick. The most common ailments of rescued sea lions are respiratory infections, or colds. A sea lion needs to hold its breath when it dives underwater for fish, but when a sea lion's nose and lungs are stuffed up, it cannot hold its breath as well.

Some of the sea lions that end up in shelters also have injuries resulting from encounters with people. These include cuts from boat propellers, wounds from tangled fishing lines, and mouth injuries from fishhooks. Animals also get hurt when they swallow trash such as plastic bags or soda-can rings. As with all wild animals, sea lions suffer when people endanger the environment in which the animals live. Understanding more about sea lions will help us to establish a balance between their needs and ours.

Pumpkin and Piper were about eight months old when they arrived at the Marine Mammal Center. Both of them were weak and underweight. Pumpkin was rescued during a winter storm and was also suffering from exposure to the cold. Most sea lions brought into rescue centers are young animals. Between birth and the age of one year, young sea lions are called *pups*. Some of the rescued sea lions are pups that became separated from their mothers too early. Others are older youngsters that were not able to find enough food on their own. The first two years in a sea lion's life are the most dangerous. Young sea lions cannot cope with bad weather conditions as well as older animals can. Also, they are not as skilled at finding food, so when food is scarce, the young are more likely to suffer.

When an animal arrives at the shelter, its species, sex, health condition, and the place where it was found are recorded on a chart. Then the animal is weighed and measured and given an identification number that is written with dye on the animal's fur. As shelter workers get to know the animal, they often give it a name as well. Finally, the new "patient" is fed and placed in an enclosure. Usually it is placed with other animals for companionship. Each enclosure has room for the animals to move about, places for resting, and a pool for swimming and getting wet. Workers keep the enclosures clean and feed the animals several times a day. Some rescued animals stay at the shelter for just a day or two. Others need several weeks or months of care before they are healthy enough to be released.

Pumpkin and Piper are California sea lions, one of five species, or kinds, of sea lions. The California sea lion is the only species in which the adult male does not have the shaggy, lion-like mane that gives sea lions their name. California sea lions have long sleek bodies, narrow snouts, bulging eyes, and small flaps over their ears. If you travel along the Pacific coast, you can often see them swimming in the surf, sitting on rocks, or resting on ocean buoys. You can also see them at zoos and aquariums, where they enter-tain visitors with their playful antics.

Most people are familiar with Cali-fornia sea lions as being the trained animals that perform in circuses and aquatic parks. Sea lions are easily trained and learn to balance and carry objects, jump through hoops, and bark on command. Except for balancing objects, these tricks are variations of behaviors that wild sea lions do every day. Sea lions also have been trained to assist divers and to perform various underwater tasks for research.

During the breeding season, Cali-fornia sea lions are found off the coast of southern California and Baja Cali-fornia in Mexico. In the nonbreeding season, they spread out along the coasts of the eastern Pacific Ocean as far north as British Columbia in Canada. California sea lions also live in the Galápagos Islands west of Ecuador and off the coast of Japan. They are the smallest sea lion species.

The Northern, or Steller, sea lion is another species seen in North Amer-ica, and it is found on the coasts of northern California north to Alaska and the Bering Strait. It is the largest kind of sea lion, with males weighing as much as 1 ton (.907 metric ton)! The other three sea lion species are the Aus-tralian, the South American, and the Hooker's, or New Zealand, sea lions. Although the five kinds of sea lions each live in a different part of the world, most of their habits and behav-iors are similar.

Male California sea lion.

As with all sea lions, adult California sea lion males are much larger than females. You can recognize an adult male by the dark brown color of his fur and by his heavy chest. Male sea lions are called *bulls*. A California sea lion bull weighs between 450 and 650 pounds (204.5–295.5 kilograms) and is from 6½ to 8½ feet (2 to 2.6 meters) long. He reaches his full size when he is about six years old. Most males, however, do not mate for the first time until they are eight years old.

A California sea lion bull has a bump, called a *sagittal crest,* on the top of his head. The sagittal crest starts growing when the male is five years old, and it is fully developed by the age of ten. The scientific name of the California sea lion, *Zalophus californianus,* comes

Female California sea lion.

from *zalophus*, a Greek word meaning "high crest," and *California*, which is the primary place where this species is found.

Female sea lions are called *cows.* They are much more slender than males. An adult California sea lion cow weighs between 120 and 250 pounds (54.5–113.6 kilograms) and is from 5 to 6½ feet (1.5 to 2 meters) long. Her coat is somewhat lighter than that of the male, and she has no bump on her head. Females are able to mate for the first time when they are about five years old.

The reproductive organs of both male and female sea lions are located inside their bodies, so until an animal has reached maturity, it is hard to tell its sex.

Sea lions belong to the order of sea mammals called Pinnipedia, a Latin word meaning "fin foot" or "wing foot." All of the animals in this order have flat flipperlike feet, and when they are swimming, they sometimes look as if they are flying through the water. Pinnipeds are found in coastal waters all over the world. Other pinnipeds at the Marine Mammal Center included elephant seals, fur seals, and harbor seals. Like Pumpkin and Piper, these animals had also been rescued from nearby beaches.

The thirty-five species of pinnipeds are divided by scientists into three families. Sea lions and fur seals belong to the family of eared seals; they all have small flaps over their ear holes. They have large front flippers and are able to walk on all four limbs. The family of earless seals includes harbor seals, monk seals, Antarctic seals, elephant seals, and others. They have no ear flaps, their front flippers are small, and the animals crawl like inchworms when they are on land. Members of this family are sometimes called "true seals." The walrus is the only member of the third family of pinnipeds. It lacks ear flaps and is distinguished by its large size and long tusks.

Harbor seal.

California sea lion.

Walrus.

Sea lions are amphibious animals, which means that they are adapted to life both in water and on land. Like all of the pinnipeds, a sea lion is an excellent swimmer with a streamlined shape that helps it to glide smoothly through the water. Twisting and turning its flexible body, a sea lion often looks like an underwater acrobat. Powerful muscles help it leap out of the water onto rocks or ledges on a beach.

Sea lions swim at speeds of 11 to 24 miles (17.7 to 38.7 kilometers) per hour, and as they swim underwater, they may be able to reach speeds of up to 30 miles (48.4 kilometers) per hour for short periods of time. Sometimes they swim rapidly across the surface of the water and leap forward like porpoises. Sea lions are also excellent bodysurfers and skillfully ride waves onto the beach when coming in to land.

As a sea lion searches for food in the ocean, it may dive up to 1,300 feet (396.2 meters) below the surface of the water and stay submerged for 10 to 15 minutes at a time. When a sea lion dives, its nostrils close so that water does not get in. Like all mammals, a sea lion needs oxygen from the air to live. Oxygen is absorbed by the blood in the lungs. When a sea lion is on the surface of the water or on land, the animal's heart beats about 85 times a minute as it circulates blood through the sea lion's body. But when a sea lion dives, its heart slows to 10 beats a minute. Blood flow is reduced to all parts of the body except to the brain and other essential organs. In this way, the sea lion's supply of oxygen lasts much longer and allows the animal to stay underwater until it needs to breathe again.

A sea lion's swimming power comes from its large flippers in the front of its body. The sea lion pushes them like oars, stroking inward and downward to propel itself through the water. The structure of the flippers is similar to that of hands and feet in land animals, but in a sea lion these appendages are specially adapted for use in the water. They are greatly flattened, and the bones are elongated and joined by dark leathery skin. The tops of the front flippers are covered with short hairs, but the bottoms are hairless.

On sunny days, sea lions sometimes hold their flippers up in the air. They may do this as a way to cool off. Blood flows closer to the surface in the flippers than it does in the body, so the blood cools more quickly when the flipper is exposed to the air.

A sea lion uses its back flippers mainly as rudders to guide and stabilize its body while moving forward through the water. The back flippers bend from the sea lion's anklebones. A sea lion can rotate its back flippers under its body. When it is on land, the animal uses the back flippers to walk, climb, or even gallop. Despite having short limbs, sea lions can move surprisingly fast on land.

The sea lion's back flippers are totally hairless, and on the top there

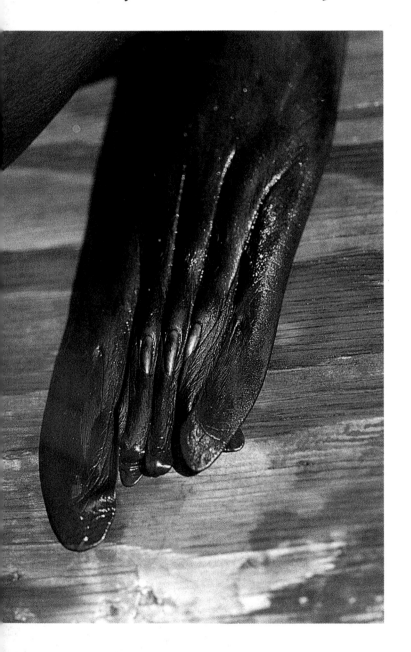

are three sharp nails. By folding the front flaps of the flippers forward, a sea lion can use these nails to scratch itself and groom its fur. Sea lions also clean themselves with their front flippers and teeth and by rubbing against pebbles or sand.

A sea lion's coat has coarse outer hairs, called *guard hairs,* and a sparse layer of soft underfur. When the fur is dry, it appears brown. When wet, the fur flattens to give the sea lion a sleek dark-colored coat. Once a year, the hairs are gradually shed, or *molted,* and replaced by new ones.

Fur helps keep a sea lion warm, but most of the animal's warmth comes from thick body fat called *blubber.* The blubber keeps a sea lion so warm that the animal has a hard time staying cool when the weather is hot. In most of the places where sea lions live, the climate is warm during much of the year. One way sea lions keep cool when they are on land is to lie in wet sand. They also make frequent trips into the water to get wet. As the water evaporates from their fur, sea lions cool off.

California sea lions.

Sea lions are very social animals and are usually found together in large groups. For California sea lions in North America the breeding season is between May and August. During that time they gather at breeding sites called *rookeries.* Rookeries are usually located on sandy beaches or rock ledges near the water. Hundreds of animals may gather at each rookery. Sea lions usually return to the same rookery year after year. (Nonbreeding sites where groups of sea lions come out of the water are called *hauling grounds.*)

Adult female California sea lions and youngsters stay in the general area of the rookeries year-round. Males travel along the coast in search of food. At the beginning of the breeding season, mature adult male sea lions return to the rookery and line up along the beach. The largest and strongest males establish territories that they defend by pushing, biting, and chasing other males that try to intrude. Bulls are able to store huge amounts of fat in their bodies. A bull that is defending his territory stays there day and night and may go for several weeks without food. Body fat provides energy to live on during this time.

Males with territories that are most

Rookery of Steller sea lions on the Oregon coast.

attractive to females will have the most opportunities to mate. Just a few males do most of the mating in a sea lion rookery. Younger males that are not successful at setting up breeding territories are called *bachelors*. These sea lions usually gather in groups on nearby beaches. As they grow older and stronger, they will be better able to compete for territories.

Several weeks after the males have set up their territories, the females arrive at the rookery and form small groups of their own. At first the females pay little attention to the males. Most of the females are pregnant from the previous mating season, and within a few days of their arrival they give birth to their pups. Each mother produces a single pup. (Twins are extremely rare.) Nearly all California sea lion pups are born during the first few weeks in June. Most of them are born at night.

About two weeks after she has given birth, a female sea lion is ready to mate again. The female leaves her pup and approaches one of the territorial bulls. Her smell tells him that she is ready to mate. After mating, the female returns to her pup and shows no further interest in the male. She will give birth to a new pup the following year.

At birth, a California sea lion pup is about 30 inches (76.9 centimeters) long and weighs about 12½ pounds (5.7 kilograms). Compared to some other mammals that are helpless at birth, a baby sea lion is quite developed. Its dark brown eyes are open, and its body is covered with coarse chestnut brown fur. Within ten to fifteen minutes after birth, the pup is able to walk and groom itself. Sea lion pups are able to swim from the time they are born, but usually they do not spend much time in the water until they are several months old.

As with other young mammals, a sea lion pup's first food is milk, which it drinks from one of its mother's four

teats. When the pup is not nursing, the teat retracts into a fold of skin. Although newly born pups may nurse several times a day, pups more than two or three weeks old nurse just once a day for about a half hour. California sea lion milk is highly nutritious; it contains about 35 percent fat and 13 percent protein. (Cow's milk has about 3.4 percent fat and 3.3 percent protein.) A mother sea lion usually stops nursing her pup when it is seven to eight months old, but some allow their youngsters to nurse until the next pup is born. A sea lion pup grows quickly, and by the time it is six months old, it weighs about 60 pounds (27.3 kilograms).

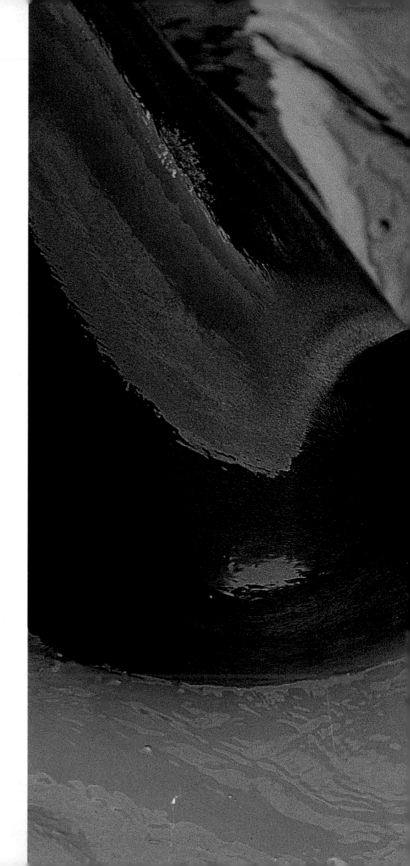

As soon as her pup is born, a mother sea lion makes loud trumpeting barks. Her pup answers these calls with tiny bleats. No two animals sound exactly alike. By repeating their calls, the mother and pup learn each other's sounds. For the first few days, the mother sea lion never leaves her pup and chases away any other sea lions that come too close. But when the pup is about four days old, the mother leaves it for the first time so she can go to sea to find food.

When the mother sea lion returns to the rookery, she calls out to her pup as soon as she gets to shore. The pup answers and the mother calls again. By calling back and forth, they quickly find each other. Then, when they get close enough to touch, they sniff and rub noses and recognize each other by their odors.

Sea lion pups are born with baby teeth, but most of these are replaced with permanent adult teeth by the time the pup is four months old. An adult sea lion has a total of thirty-four to thirty-six teeth, with ten incisors in the front (six in the upper jaw and four in the lower jaw), plus two long canines and ten to twelve cheek teeth on each side. Sea lions do not chew their food. Instead, they swallow it whole. Their pointed teeth are used for catching and grasping their prey. In males, the canines are extra large and are also used for biting opponents during fights. The tongues of sea lions are short with a notch at the tip. Scientists believe that sea lions do not have a strong sense of taste.

The size and condition of a sea lion's teeth can be used to determine the approximate age of the animal. The teeth of wild sea lions show that they may live to be fifteen years old or more. In captivity, some sea lions have lived as long as thirty years.

In the wild, the main food of California sea lions is squid and octopus, but they also eat such small fish as herring and anchovies. A young sea lion begins to eat solid food when it is several months old. It may first learn to catch small fish in tide pools at the edge of the sea. But soon the sea lion follows its mother into the ocean and hunts for food there. Young animals learn to hunt by trial and error, and with practice, they gradually become expert fish catchers.

At the shelter, the animals are fed several times a day. A year-old sea lion eats about 5 to 10 pounds (2.3 to 4.5 kilograms) of fish each day. Adult females eat about 25 pounds (11.4 kilograms) and bulls up to 60 pounds (27.2 kilograms). Most of the rescued sea lions are fed fish, but young animals that cannot eat solid food are started with special sea lion "milk shakes," a mixture of ground-up fish, water, and nutrients. These are fed directly into the sea lion's stomach through long tubes.

Sea lions in rescue centers are not tame. Thick clothing and large wooden boards help protect people from being bitten when they are working in the sea lion enclosure.

Sea lions rarely drink water because they get all the water they need from the food they eat. However, many of the animals that come into the shelter are thirsty because they have not had enough to eat. They are given a mixture of sugar water, vitamins, and minerals right away to help restore their body fluids.

Wild sea lions and seals have often been found with stones in their stomachs. Some people think that the weight of the stones helps to stabilize the animals as they swim, or that the sea lions and seals swallow the stones to help break up food or to kill harmful worms that live in their stomachs. No one really knows, and until further study is done, this strange behavior remains a mystery.

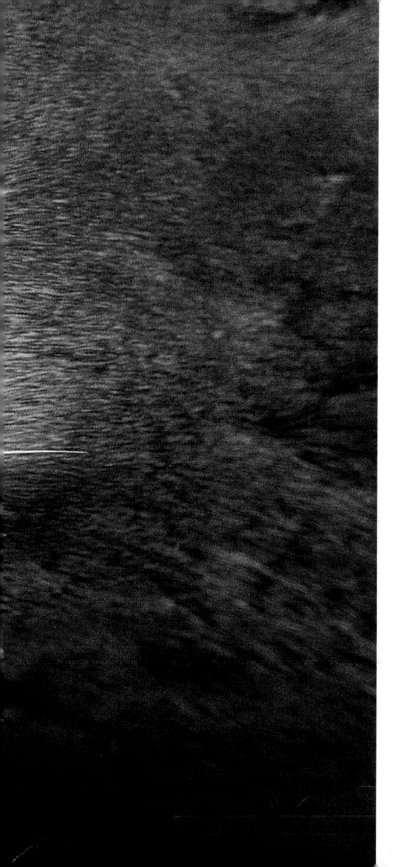

Sea lions nap both during the day and at night and can sleep in or out of the water. In the water they usually lie on one side, sometimes with one flipper pointed upward. On land they often tuck their flippers underneath themselves. Sea lions usually sleep together, often forming huge piles of bodies. At the shelter, Pumpkin and Piper often cuddled together to sleep. Pups do not have as much body fat as adults. When they cluster together, it helps them keep warm.

When the mothers of sea lion pups go out to sea, the pups come together in groups called *pods*. Pods may consist of as few as five or six or as many as two hundred pups.

Sea lion pups are active and curious and spend a great deal of time playing with one another and exploring. They chase one another, play follow the leader, and tussle in mock battles. For young males, play fighting is preparation for actual fighting they will have to do as adults in order to establish breeding territories. Both pups and adults pick up objects such as stones and seaweed and toss them about as if playing a game of catch. Sea lions also have been observed chasing their air bubbles underwater. Scientists do not know why they do this. At the shelter, Pumpkin and Piper sometimes played chasing and pushing games with each other.

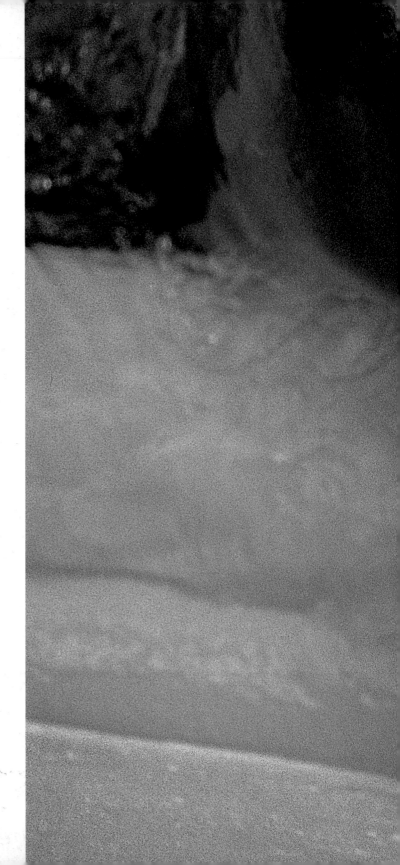

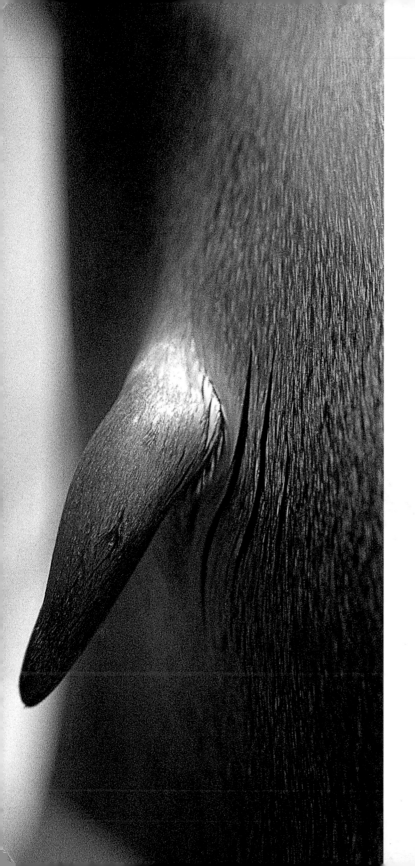

Ear of a California sea lion.

Both in the wild and in captivity, the sea lions' barking makes the places where they live extremely noisy. Bulls use vocal signals to identify themselves, to advertise their location, and to declare their social status. They also bark as a warning to intruders on their territories. Sea lion mothers and their pups use sounds to locate each other when they are separated and when they are with other sea lions. A sea lion's sense of hearing is good, and loud barking helps individual sea lions to communicate with one another easily even when they are on opposite sides of a rookery or hauling ground.

The large eyes of sea lions help them to see underwater when the light is dim. Although sea lions do not have sharp vision, they are able to detect large shapes and rapid movements. In addition to their normal eyelids, sea lions have a transparent eyelid called the *nictitating membrane.* It protects the eye from blowing sand when the animal is on the beach. As with other animals, tears moisten the sea lion's eyes. Because a sea lion has no tear ducts, the tears run down its face when it is out of the water.

One of the sea lion's most developed senses is that of touch. When sea lions meet, they often rub their bodies together and touch noses. A sea lion has long sensitive whiskers called *vibrissae* on its nose. These whiskers are highly flexible, and the sea lion can move them from a folded-back position against the face to a nearly forward position. The whiskers can feel even the slightest movements. In the water, a sea lion uses them to detect the vibrations made by a swimming fish, which it then locates and catches.

Killer whale.

Most of the islands and secluded beaches where sea lions come out of the water are so difficult to reach that the animals are usually safe from land predators. But if one of the sea lions detects danger, it gives a sharp alarm call and all the sea lions dash for the sea. The water, however, can be a much more dangerous place. There, the sea lions must watch out for sharks and killer whales. Although killer whales are aquatic animals, they sometimes pursue sea lions right up onto a beach. In the Arctic, Steller sea lions are also hunted by polar bears.

Sea lions have been hunted by people for thousands of years. In the eighteenth and nineteenth centuries, the thick blubber of sea lions was melted to make lamp oil. Sea lions also have been killed for their meat and hides. Since 1972, when the Marine Mammal Protection Act was passed by Congress, sea lions that live along the coast of the United States have been protected in their breeding places. From that time, the number of sea lions has grown every year. The current population of California sea lions is about 100,000.

Tiger shark (top);
polar bear (bottom).

After two months at the Marine Mammal Center, Pumpkin and Piper were ready to go back to the wild. Their bodies were plump, and they were eating well on their own. Now that they were strong and healthy again, they would have a good chance of surviving out in the ocean.

Before each animal is released from a shelter, a permanent identification tag provided by the National Marine Fisheries Service is attached to one of the back flippers. The tag helps people identify the sea lion when it is seen in the wild or if it is rescued again. Tags also help scientists to study the movements of sea lions and to monitor their activities.

On the day of their release, Pumpkin and Piper were awakened early. Then they were herded into a large animal carrier and loaded onto a truck. Although some rescued animals are released directly into the water from boats, others, like Pumpkin and Piper, are taken to beaches where there are other sea lions nearby.

At the beach, shelter workers carried the container with the two sea lions in it across the sand. The young animals could hear sea gulls squawking overhead and could smell the salty air. When the door of their carrier was opened, Pumpkin and Piper cautiously peeked out. At first they seemed reluctant to leave the security of their temporary home and the people who had cared for them. Soon, however, they climbed out and took off toward the lapping waves.

Pumpkin and Piper were strong and seemed sure of themselves as they raced toward the sea. When they reached the water's edge, they dove into the surf and began swimming toward the horizon.

Once again, the two young sea lions were free. Just a few months earlier they had been too weak to find food for themselves. Now, with the help of the staff at the Marine Mammal Center, they had been given a second chance. With luck, Pumpkin and Piper will find other sea lions and grow up to produce youngsters of their own.

Marine mammal centers help sea animals to recover from illness and injury. They also provide an opportunity for people to learn about these mammals and their natural habitat. You may be able to see wild sea lions if you visit the west coast of the United States and Canada. You can also enjoy watching these playful animals in many zoos and aquatic parks. The more we know about sea lions, the better we will be at helping to protect them and the places they live.

Index